AF575193

Other books by the author:

The Old Cathedral
1965 (2nd edition, 1980)
The Story of Old Ste. Genevieve
1967 (2nd edition, 1973; 3rd edition, 1976; 4th edition, 1987)
The Oregon Trail Revisited
1972 (2nd edition, 1978; 3rd edition, 1983; 4th edition, 1988)
History of the Hazelwood School District
1977
Legacy; The Sverdrup Story
1978 (2nd printing, 1987)
Leif Sverdrup; Engineer Soldier At His Best
1980 (2nd printing, 1986)
Maps of the Oregon Trail
1982 (2nd edition, 1983)
Impressions of the Santa Fe Trail; A Contemporary Diary
1988
Challenge: The Sverdrup Story Continues
1988

IMAGES

OF ◊ THE ◊ SANTA ◊ FE ◊ TRAIL

To a couple of good neighbors - Richard & Kathy [illegible] with best wishes
Gregory M. Franzwa
April 18, 1994

Photographs and Text by
Gregory M. Franzwa

Foreword by
Gaylord Nelson

The Patrice Press
St. Louis, Missouri

First printing, August 1988

Library of Congress Cataloging-in-Publishing Data

Franzwa, Gregory M.
Images of the Santa Fe Trail.

1. Santa Fe Trail—Pictorial works. 2. Santa Fe Trail—History. I. Title.
F786.F793 1988 978 88-23868
ISBN 0-935284-60-5
ISBN 0-935284-61-3 (pbk.)

Published by
The Patrice Press
1701 South Eighth Street
St. Louis MO 63104

Printed in the United States of America

To Molly Sverdrup,
friend of a lifetime

FOREWORD

If ever America needed her historic trails, that time is now. Like the Oregon, Lewis and Clark, Mormon Pioneer, and Iditerod trails, the Santa Fe Trail now has won its recognition from the government of the United States as a National Historic Trail. Thus we have acknowledged the great pioneering efforts made by the people, Hispanic as well as Anglo, who wedded the American Southwest to the United States.

It is a history as romantic as it is politically meaningful. So now, perhaps, the educational establishment of this nation will be able to expand its focus to include more of the country's western trails.

This book proves something: if history is properly packaged, it can be great fun. To browse through these photographs and read Gregory M. Franzwa's delightful captions is just that, great fun. And it is easy to get into the spirit of his exciting adventure, shared with the National Park Service, as he explored the old trail and talked with the wonderful people who live near it—the men and women who in fact have been protecting it for much of their lives.

We can feel the cold raindrops propelled by a vicious Kansas wind as the survey party stands atop Indian Mound. We can feel the warmth of people like Dale Eichenauer, who dug the ox chains of some long-dead freighter from the ruts of the Santa Fe Trail which course through his ranch. We can feel the holiness of the silent churches, still standing watch over nearly abandoned communities deep in New Mexico.

Because of this book, many people will seek new adventures in exploring the old Santa Fe Trail. I hope, most sincerely, that they leave it as they found it, that they respect the rights and privacy of the people who own trail lands. And I hope they will come away with a new sense of appreciation of those courageous men and women who found a highway to national greatness in the old Santa Fe Trail.

—Gaylord Nelson,
The Wilderness Society
July 15, 1988

ACKNOWLEDGMENTS

Lisa Taylor of The Patrice Press helped with the design of this book, after a period of intensive research. I am most appreciative of her efforts and of her dedication to the task. I am pleased, also, with the work of Tom Stewart's Silver Image, Ltd., the lab which processed the film and printed the negatives.

I am flattered by the willingness of Gaylord Nelson, the great Wisconson conservationist, former United States senator and author of America's Scenic Trails System, to draft the foreword to this book. Marc Simmons, the great guru of the Santa Fe Trail, has proofread the manuscript and pulled out some awful klinkers. He is not only the trail's foremost scholar and most prolific author, he is a nice guy, too. Another valued friend is Leo Oliva, my companion on the National Park Service expedition of 1988 and himself a renowned Santa Fe Trail scholar. Dr. Oliva, like Dr. Simmons, helped whip this manuscript into shape.

Finally, I am grateful to my colleague and friend, Dr. Betty Burnett, editor of The Patrice Press, for her careful perusal of the manuscript and help in photo selection.

All the black-and-white photographs were taken with a Minolta 7000 35mm camera, on Plus X film.

—Gregory M. Franzwa
July 1988

IMAGES
OF◇THE◇SANTA◇FE◇TRAIL

INTRODUCTION

In 1978 Congress amended the National Trails Systems Act to include four new National Historic Trails in the West: Oregon, Lewis & Clark, Iditerod, and Mormon Pioneer trails. Conspicuously absent was the Santa Fe Trail.

That national error of omission was corrected on May 8, 1987, when President Ronald Reagan signed the act designating the Santa Fe Trail as a National Historic Trail.

The National Park Service, as administering agency, then assumed responsibility for a thorough study of the trail, from which will emerge, in mid-1989, a comprehensive trail plan, an inventory of historic sites along the old trail, and a book of maps showing the route of the trail overlaid on a base of contemporary road maps, from mid-Missouri to Santa Fe.

The Patrice Press, which intended to publish *Maps of the Santa Fe Trail* as a companion volume to its much-acclaimed *Maps of the Oregon Trail,* offered to share field time with the National Park Service study team, and to make copies of the pages of the new map book available as a bona fide component of the study. That offer was accepted.

The author and editor Betty Burnett made a preliminary field trip to Santa Fe early in March 1988. Then followed four major field trips with the National Park Service team, beginning March 16 and ending on May 22, 1988.

At every major historic site along the way, at the major stream crossings, and wherever pronounced rut swales were visible, photographs were taken. Solo trips were taken in pre-dawn darkness to capture some sights at sunrise. Long tripod exposures were sometimes made in deepening twilight. The photographs on these pages are the best of the hundreds of exposures made.

But before embarking on the photographic journey, a look should be taken at the historic trail.

In the summer of 1821 a farmer living near Fayette, Missouri, decided that the time was right for a trading expedition to Santa Fe, then part of Mexico. The time most assuredly was not right, as Spain long had looked to venturesome Yankee traders as hostiles. But on June 25, William Becknell inserted an ad in the *Missouri Intelligencer,* published in the booming Missouri River town of Franklin, calling for a company of men to accompany him on a trading expedition with the Indians. However, many scholars feel that he really intended to go to Santa Fe.

Had Becknell been an astute historian, he would have known that a Santa Fe expedition would have very little chance of success. Not that American goods weren't desired in the old city; they certainly were. But Spain entertained the constant fear that it was only a matter of time before the northerners made a move to annex New Mexico to the United States. Hence, traders who had ventured to that land in prior years often languished in Chihuahua dungeons for months and years, and never realized anything but grief for their trouble.

But because history sometimes takes some strange turns, William Becknell today is remembered as the founder of the Santa Fe Trail. Less than three months after he had placed his ad in the *Intelligencer,* and a few days after his mule train trotted to the west, Mexico gained her independence from Spain. Becknell began his journey on the first day of September. For the first time, American traders would be welcomed in Santa Fe.

It is uncertain where William Becknell met his comrades to begin the journey. It could have been his farm, near his unsuccessful salt distillation operation at Boone's Lick, or possibly he departed from Franklin and followed the old road northwest to the ferry landing. It is known that he crossed the Missouri River to the spring at Arrow Rock—not then a city but just that, a rock—and headed west from there.

Becknell left any vestige of Anglo civilization at Fort Osage, northeast of the present city of Independence, Missouri, and headed west from there. He followed the Arkansas River to what is now eastern Colorado, then turned south up the Purgatoire. He probably crossed over Raton Pass, then continued to San Miguel and northwest up the Fishhook to Santa Fe. He arrived in the City of the Holy Faith on November 16, and his trade goods were sold quickly to delighted buyers at enormous profit.

Becknell returned, not over the Mountain Branch, but over a flat shortcut along the Cimarron River, later named the Jornada—pathway—sixty miles without water, wood, or grass. That later became the main route of the Santa Fe Trail.

Many accounts have stated that Becknell returned to Arrow Rock, cut the thongs of rawhide pouches and watched the welcoming committee gape as the horde of silver dollars cascaded into the stone gutters. Good story, but Arrow Rock had no stone gutters then. In fact, it wasn't even platted until 1829. That incident could have happened in Franklin, however, when Becknell returned on January 30, 1822.

The Missouri adventurer wasn't the only man to have a good idea coupled with good luck. Two weeks after the Becknell train arrived in Santa Fe another group of traders showed up. The great trail was on its way.

Growth of tonnage on the trail was relatively slow through the 1820s and 1830s, but after 1846, when the Spanish-Mexican fears were realized and the United States did indeed take the Southwest by force of arms, trading on the trail reached enormous proportions. It was big business.

But there was trouble on the trail. The Indians considered the West their land by right of prior occupancy. The traders didn't quarrel with that; they merely wanted to pass through. Treaties had been effected with some of the tribes, but much hostility ranged south of the Arkansas. These were not the begging, stock-stealing Indians of the Oregon Trail, but sadistic torturers and killers, determined to frighten the white man from the Santa Fe Trail.

There was some justification to their case. The whites

made no attempt to carry food or forage with them; they lived off the land of the Indian, who saw the consequent dimishment of the buffalo as life-threatening.

As more and more caravans were attacked, the clamor arose for federal protection along the old highway. Forts were built, soldiers came to the West to pursue and subjugate the Indian. Mindless massacres of whites were avenged with mindless massacres of more Indians, and little by little the red man lost the war.

Enabling legislation gave entrepreneurs a leg up on the financial difficulties of spanning the continent with steel rails, and with the end of the Civil War building started in earnest. The Kansas Pacific penetrated first, not along the trail but north of it. The railheads, however, changed the route of the trail drastically. Soon the Atchison, Topeka & Santa Fe raced directly down the old trace, following William Becknell's historic route over Raton Pass, and by 1880 the Santa Fe Trail was history.

The route of the trail, as selected by the National Park Service, was difficult to determine. There is no question but what the trade flowed as much southwest to northeast as it did northeast to southwest. There probably were as many Mexican traders on the trail as Americans; as many caravans originated in Santa Fe as in Missouri.

But almost all of them made round trips, carrying goods from Missouri to Santa Fe, and returning with furs and silver to Missouri. Therefore, the National Park Service declaration shows the old trail beginning on the site of Franklin, or rather what is left of the site. Most of it was in the Missouri River by 1828, but the trade had by that time moved to Independence, and a little later expanded to Westport, the parent of Kansas City (which gobbled up its own mother in the 1870s.)

Those were the eastern ganglia until just before and during the Civil War. Then, the vicious border warfare perpetrated by white ruffians forced the trade to Fort Leavenworth, where armed escorts could guide the traders through territory plagued by people whose mindless brutality made the Indians look like good old boys.

But before that period the caravans either moved south out of Independence, then west across the Missouri line, or west through Westport, then southwest through Olathe. The two roads joined near little Gardner, Kansas, and proceeded through Palmyra, now Baldwin City, and on to the Neosho at Council Grove. There, in a sylvan setting, the traders did the last of their reorganization, often joining with others awaiting reinforcements there, and headed into the country of the hostiles.

They passed Diamond Spring, then Lost Spring, negotiated a hellacious crossing of Cottonwood Creek, then arrived at the Little Arkansas. A few days later they crossed Walnut Creek and arrived at the river which would shelter them for many miles, the Arkansas. Past present Great Bend they came into view of Pawnee Rock, a startling landmark rising abruptly from the Kansas plain. If it were the 1860s and if the day were clear, the garrison flag from Fort Larned could be seen from the top of that rock.

Past present Dodge City rolled the caravans, the traders often leaving their broad, flat highway to examine two deep holes in the earth. They were located where an early caravan fell upon hard times and had to cache their goods until they could go on to Santa Fe and return with a new stock of mules to haul it to pay dirt. "The Caches" were there until early in the twentieth century, when local ranching operations gradually filled in the cavities, and now nobody knows exactly where they were.

A few traders crossed the Arkansas below present Dodge City, but the majority left the sustaining valley near the present town of Cimarron, to head southwest. Some continued on to the long-vanished Chouteau's Island, near present Lakin, Kansas, to cross there. Either way, they were faced with big trouble, for they were now on the feared Jornada, or "waterscrape." About the only people who really liked the Jornada were the Indians, who found it a very good place to add to their scalp collections.

As the traders approached the long-awaited Cimarron, that treeless and tempermental watercourse, they came across a hole in the ground from which issued fairly decent water. In ranching days this became know as Wagon Bed Spring, but in the early years it was simply the Lower Spring.

Then they saw a sliver of land laying on the horizon like a lead pencil; near its point—the "Point of Rocks"—was another spring, also on the Cimarron.

That spring, the Middle Spring, still flows, impounded now by beavers. (Yes, there are beavers in Kansas.)

Crossing the Cimarron at a wooded sandspit called Willow Bar, the traders then came to the Upper Spring, later known as Flag Spring. The other two springs were fairly sedate; this one was and still is spectacular. Surrounded by towering rocks, it is now dammed to a sequestered pool, a setting so peaceful it is impossible to imagine the violence surrounding the place when the Comanches and Kiowas were the landlords and the traders were the tenants who paid their rent with blood and hair.

Passing Cold Spring, the Rabbit Ears came in view. Looking not the least bit like rabbit ears, they were named not by someone with a dizzy imagination, but for an Indian chief of that name.

Far ahead was Sierra Grande, sometimes snow-capped, and, to the left, Round Mound, now known as Mount Clayton. It is a fairly symmetrical cone, fitting its name no better than Rabbit Ears.

The trail crosses the Canadian River the only place it could, at a shallow crossing of solid rock. To the left a canyon up to several hundred feet deep extended for more than one hundred miles. To the right is deep sand for many miles. But here it was ideal.

Then came a landmark about which there could be no guessing, Wagon Mound. Looking for all the world like a huge freight wagon perched atop a pyramidical pedestal, Wagon Mound was in view for three or four days, as the wagons ground toward it at the rate of fifteen to eighteen miles a day.

There could be no doubt about it now—the teamsters were in another world. There is no doubt about it today. The Anglo culture had been replaced with the Hispanic. The settlements were formed of adobe, not frame. There was a dryness to the air, making the warmth of the sun tolerable. There was a warmth of the welcome, too, as uninhibited New Mexicans let the gringos know they appreciated their efforts.

Because of the Sangre de Cristo Mountains, the old roadway had to go far to the south of Santa Fe, through the settlement of San Miguel, before it could turn to the northwest to enter the fabled city of Santa Fe. On that last stretch the travelers were able to view the ancient pueblo of Pecos, long since abandoned. The last barrier, Glorieta Pass, was destined to become the site of a pivotal battle of the Civil War.

Finally the weary travelers caught sight of their dusty destination from the heights above Santa Fe. That was an exhilarating experience, never to be forgotten by any trader.

Since the Santa Fe Trail was almost always a round-trip experience, the National Park Service survey party returned to the north by way of the Mountain Branch, rather than ask the reader-traveler to vault from Santa Fe to western Kansas to start the last leg.

Things had gotten so bad in the Jornada that during and after the Civil War the route was virtually abandoned in favor of the fortified Mountain Branch. The traders swapped the extra eighty-five miles for a lot of security and a tough pull over the Raton, made a little easier by Uncle Dick Wootton's famous toll road.

Traders returning to "the States" from Santa Fe would leave the way they came in, all the way to La Junta, or present-day Watrous, New Mexico. This was named not so much for the junction of the Cimarron Cutoff and the Mountain Branch, but for the confluence of the Mora and Sapello creeks.

There they would turn off to the north and, in later years, pass through Fort Union. They had one major creek to cross, Ocate, but it was rarely a difficult crossing. They passed the point of the mesa and continued north to the town of Rayado. There they could see the homes of legendary westerner Kit Carson and land baron Lucien Maxwell.

Then came the town of Cimarron, where Maxwell had his mill and where a bona fide hotel, the St. James, offered lodging to people able to afford it. (The same is true today.) Another hostelry, larger, older, and a lot more impressive, was ahead. Almost to the Raton, Clifton House—a three-story, fort-like building plus its outbuildings—was a small city unto itself.

In the pass proper, in later years, was Richens Lacy ("Uncle Dick") Wootton, proprietor of a much-improved toll road over the last major barrier between Santa Fe and the States. From the crest the travelers got a stupendous view of the Spanish Peaks, outriders of the Sangre de Cristo. They came off the high ground to Trinidad, still a Hispanic-flavored community, then followed Purgatoire ("Picketwire") Creek to Hole in the

Rock at the head of Timpas Creek. Moving past Iron Spring, they finally arrived at the oasis known as Bent's Fort or, in later years as today, Bent's Old Fort.

Here, west of Las Animas, they got a breath of Anglo civilization. Then they arrived at the government's Fort Lyon, built to provide protection along the road.

They would then cross into present-day Kansas, pass the site of Fort Aubry, and come into view of Indian Mound, the tall, earthen promontory believed to be a natural feature (although some feel it might have been built by Auguste P. Chouteau, a fur trader during the first years of the nineteenth century). This overlooks the upper crossing of the Arkansas, and the westernmost commencement of the Cimarron Cutoff.

There is a paucity of photographs of ruts in this collection, simply because the ruts of the Santa Fe Trail are almost impossible to capture on black-and-white film. Not that they aren't there—miles and miles of them are there, awaiting the viewer. Some are deeply eroded but most are simply linear depressions in the unbroken sod of the prairies. It requires binocular vision to see them properly.

Most of the ruts, particularly in the Indian country, are four abreast. It took far less time to form a breastworks of wagons by traveling this way than in a single line, and time was of the essence in defending against Indian attack. Some, particularly in national grasslands, extend unbroken for dozens of miles.

There is a mystique about this Santa Fe Trail, and it doesn't require either a dreamer or a historian to feel it. The aura may come in old Franklin, Fort Osage, Independence, or Westport. But if it hasn't hit by then it surely will by Council Grove. The feeling is deep and solid, and, fair warning, once it hits, it will never let go.

THE PHOTOGRAPHS

The *Missouri Intelligencer,* mid-Missouri's first newspaper, is commemorated by this marker on the site of Old Franklin. This was the paper which carried the notice by William Becknell of the first legal Santa Fe Trail expedition, which left the vicinity on September 1, 1821. Much of Old Franklin, which was across the Missouri River from Boonville, tumbled into that stream in the late 1820s.

H. Denny Davis, publisher of the Fayette *Advertiser,* stands at the marker commemorating the site of Cooper's Fort. Some feel the old fort, which was active during the War of 1812, was located about where the small building is situated, above the sign. The site is near the eastern landing for the Arrow Rock ferry.

If William Becknell's New Mexican silver clattered into the stone gutters, as the story goes, it was not here at Arrow Rock, but at long-disappeared Franklin, across the river. The town of Arrow Rock was not founded until several years after Becknell's return from Santa Fe.

The Huston Tavern, Arrow Rock, was built in 1834 and restored in 1987-88 by the state of Missouri.

The third day of the National Park Service's Santa Fe Trail expedition was greeted with a chill rain mixed with sleet and snow. The upper floor of Arrow Rock's Huston Tavern was a good place to be.

William Becknell and his fellow adventurers rendezvoused at the spring at Arrow Rock on his history-making first legal trading expedition to Santa Fe. The spring still flows, but now from a pipe imbedded in the concrete and stone foundation of this little pavilion.

Cemeteries are good places to find the swales of the Santa Fe Trail, because they are never cultivated. This cemetery is in the little town of Grand Pass, Missouri, where the swale is broad and deep.

In 1825 the Sibley survey party started work from a point about a mile south of Fort Osage. That frontier post has been carefully reconstructed by the Jackson County, Missouri, Parks Department. Extensive archaeological excavation revealed the siting and footprints of most of the buildings. The Missouri River is barely visible in the background through the trees.

Nothing remains of the Blue Mill of the Aull brothers but a few foundation stones still clinging to the bank of the Blue River, in Jackson County, Missouri.

Pioneer Park in old Westport (now in Kansas City) honors three of the great men of the West: John Calvin McCoy, foreground, who platted Westport; Alexander Majors, behind him, the most famous freighter of the Santa Fe Trail; and Jim Bridger, one of the greatest of the mountain men, right. The sculpture was dedicated in October 1987.

The home of Alexander Majors, 8201 State Line Road, faces the state of Kansas. Just across the border thousands of oxen and wagons were assembled for duty on the Santa Fe Trail.

There is a deep swale in Minor Park, in the southwestern part of Kansas City, visible from Red Bridge Road just west of the Big Blue River. A DAR marker has been placed in the depression, made by tens of thousands of wagons bound for Santa Fe and Oregon.

This remarkable swale of the Santa Fe Trail leads from the Missouri River landing to the high ground upon which Fort Leavenworth stands. The smoothness of the cut indicates that the path had been at least partially spaded out to ease the way of the wagons.

The Grinter House, built in 1857, overlooks the site of the Grinter Ferry, which carried the Santa Fe wagons from Fort Leavenworth across the Kansas River en route to the main trail. Moses Grinter started his ferry operation here, in present Kansas City, Kansas, in January 1831.

One of the most appreciated stage stations on the Santa Fe Trail was the Mahaffie House, currently owned and operated by the city of Olathe, Kansas. The stage line extended from Westport to Santa Fe and stopped here once a month. The house, which is open to the public, was built in 1865.

Three great swales of the Santa Fe Trail cut through this field in Black Jack Park, southeast of Baldwin City, Kansas.

The Sibley survey party of 1825-27 came through Black Jack Park, and this is one of two stones which mark its passage. The Sibley group, however, did their marking with short-lived earthen mounds. This rock was cut by a landowner sometime after World War II and placed in the park.

Just north of Baldwin City is a small triangle of land called Trail Park. This road, heading northwest, forms one leg of the triangle. It is on top of the old Santa Fe Trail.

Atop Simmons Point, a high knob in the western portion of Douglas County, Kansas, stands this recently abandoned building, once a stage station, but now staring hollow-eyed at an uncertain future.

Santa Fe traders had an uncanny ability to find just the right places to cross difficult streams. The ford of Dragoon Creek, a few miles west of Burlingame, Kansas, has a smooth rock bottom.

he remains of the McGee-Harris stage station, west f Overbrook, Kansas, are at the west end of a deeply utted dirt lane. The site, once bustling with life, is now hostly.

Between the fords of Dragoon and Soldier creeks is this lonely grave, that of Dragoon Samuel Hunt, who died on the Santa Fe Trail in 1835. The marker was erected by the War Department in the 1930s.

The Hays House is still an active (and very good) Council Grove restaurant, right on the Santa Fe Trail one block from the crossing of the Neosho River.

Kansas State Historical Society

Built by Malcolm Conn in 1858, the old Conn's Store is probably the most important building in Council Grove. It is on the southeast corner of Main (the Santa Fe Trail) and Neosho streets. In the late 1860s Conn sold out to Shamleffer and James, shortly before the historic photograph above was taken.

This little country school, now abandoned, stands south of Council Grove. It was new when the trail was old.

Diamond Spring is fourteen miles west of Council Grove. In trail days it was referred to as the "diamond of the plains." Now it rises beneath the concrete cap in the center of this picture, and part of the overflow falls out the end of the white plastic pipe at the right.

Jerry O'Connor, manager of the Diamond Creek Ranch, rides to meet the National Park Service survey team at the Diamond Spring. He is talking with Donald Cress, a local guide from Council Grove. Others, from left, are Jere Krakow and Les Vilda, a Nebraska historian.

This old barn is on the historic Six Mile Ranch, named because it was six miles down the Santa Fe Trail from Diamond Spring. Here, too, is the crossing of Six Mile Creek, in a rock-floored dry wash of the creek.

Lost Spring is about a day's wagon drive from Diamond Spring. The spring today rises from the base of this gnarled tree near the blacktop access road and flows down to the creek beneath a cover of watercress.

Usually when ruts erode, it is due to washing action of precipitation. But here, a few of miles southwest of Durham, Kansas, is the "blowout"—a stretch of the trail perhaps a half-mile long which has been blown away by the relentless winds of Kansas.

Grass-grown ruts are exceedingly difficult to photograph with color film, and almost impossible in black-and-white. Yet, these deep swales on the farm of Jim and Mim Nelson managed to show up faintly. They are in McPherson County, Kansas.

Bob Gray, a strapping six-footer from McPherson, Kansas, illustrates the enormous size of this cottonwood, growing smack in the trail leading to the crossing of the Little Arkansas River. The trail ruts go around it, indicating that it is more than 120 years old.

Just west of the crossing of the Little Arkansas was a stone corral of massive dimensions: 200 feet by 400 feet, several feet high, and with walls fifteen inches thick. Not one rock is left; the nineteenth-century rancher who owned the acreage sold them all. But a half-mile to the west is this wall, laid up with the same kind of stone.

Four miles west of Lyons is the well of Bill Mathewson, who operated a ranch there in the 1850s. He was the original "Buffalo Bill." The modern highway bridge crossing Cow Creek is in the center of this photo, and is believed to have been built over the Santa Fe Trail crossing.

Ralph Hathaway is a rancher living near Chase, Kansas. He takes such pride in the deep swales which cross his land that they have come to be called "Ralph's Ruts," so proclaimed by a sign on the highway.

This tall water tower is situated on the highest point of the grounds of the state hospital in Larned. The hill drops off abruptly to the Pawnee Fork and the crossing of the Santa Fe Trail. The survey party was warmed by the morning sun as they headed back to the automobiles to continue the exploration.

The excitement for the traders rose a bit when Pawnee Rock came into view. Once a much taller prairie landmark, it has been reduced by quarrying. Indians bent upon ambush once lurked here; now it is a place of tranquility. Pawnee Rock is west of Great Bend, Kansas.

When the Fort Larned Historical Society turned over the site of old Fort Larned to the National Park Service, it had to remove its own artifacts which had been on display there. Generous donations from local citizens funded the expansive Santa Fe Trail Center, near Larned. Here is its stone springhouse and windmill, a fitting background for the display of historic barbed wire wrapped around this stone post.

Kansas, like Nebraska, was the home of many sod houses. This one stands behind the Santa Fe Trail Center.

Fort Larned is a fascinating restoration on the Kansas plains west of Larned.

The old fort was in use as the headquarters for a large ranching operation before it was taken over by the Fort Larned Historical Society. The National Park Service refurbished and refurnished this row of officers' quarters.

The last building to be added to old Fort Larned was this blockhouse, completed in the spring of 1988. It is a total reconstruction, and a faithful one.

This sentry box tops the Fort Larned blockhouse.

Santa Fe traders passing through Kansas identified three places as "Point of Rocks" in that state alone. One, west of Dodge City, was blasted away by senseless highway wideners in the 1980s. Another, the famous one, overlooks the Middle Spring near the Oklahoma border. This one, virtually unknown, is along the Santa Fe railroad west of Pierceville.

This eminence, Indian Mound, overlooks the upper crossing of the Arkansas River near Lakin, Kansas. The 1988 survey party visited it as a tremendous electrical storm was building to the southeast. A cold April wind lashed the area, turning the scattered raindrops into bullets.

THE CIMARRON CUTOFF

On the Cimarron Cutoff, south of the Arkansas, was th feared Jornada. This was an Indian-infested, waterles stretch of some sixty-five miles. Traders considered th route worth the danger, for it saved nearly a week extra traveling had they taken the Mountain Branch the Santa Fe Trail.

The survey party was escorted by Ron and Karla French of Ulysses, Kansas, to the spot where they believe the original Upper Spring once refreshed the Santa Fe traders. Like everything else around the Cimarron these days, it is totally dry because the water table has been lowered by extensive irrigation. Jere Krakow throws brush from the hole as Leo Oliva records the procedure on videotape. Watching are, from left, Linda Peters, Betty Burnett, Karla and Ron French, and Paul Bentrup.

At first it appeared as a slim line on the right horizon, like a slender pencil lying on the earth. But it was a landmark mesa for the Santa Fe traders, the famed Point of Rocks.

A fine road has been built to the top of Point of Rocks, where this dramatic view of the Cimarron can still thrill the traveler. The trail passed in the middle ground. That is not water in the river; it is sand. Most of the trees are now dead, victims of the lowering water table, and soon the area will have the same aspect it held in trading days, with not a tree in sight.

The Santa Fe traders approaching Point of Rocks always refreshed themselves at the Middle Spring, now a series of pools created by beaver dams.

The U.S. Forest Service has done a good job of preserving the ruts of the Santa Fe Trail through the Cimarron National Grasslands, northeast of Elkhart, Kansas. The rut swales sometimes extend unbroken for miles, and hikers are always welcomed.

Lawyer Ed White's Cessna proved an ideal platform for studying the ruts of the Santa Fe Trail. These, northeast of Elkhart, Kansas, appear along a country road, and seem to have been scratched into the earth by the fingers of a giant hand.

Autograph Rock is on the ranch of Dan and Carol Sharp, north of Boise City, Oklahoma.

Jesus M. Pacheco signed in, going and coming; his name appears on Autograph Rock in three other places.

Flag Springs, also known as Upper Springs, feeds this pool in a sylvan setting on the Oklahoma Panhandle prairie.

Kit Carson built Camp Nichols between the forks of the Carrizozo Creek to protect Santa Fe traders who were being harassed by Indians. It served its purpose nobly, but only for the summer months of 1865, after which it was abandoned. The foundations are sharp and distinct from land or from the air.

The most elusive of the Santa Fe Trail alternates under study was the trace pioneered by veteran trader Francis X. Aubry. It took off from the Mountain Branch near Lakin, Kansas, and proceeded down through western Kansas, eastern Colorado, and joined the Cimarron Cutoff in the Oklahoma Panhandle. The survey party, with its local guides, often had to stand on their vehicles to try to spot the rut swales. This unsuccessful search took place in the southeastern corner of Colorado.

Santa Fe traders were not far into New Mexico before they caught sight of the noted landmark, Rabbit Ears Mountain. The formation doesn't look like a rabbit's ears; it doesn't even look like a mountain. It was named for an Indian chief.

Imogene Thoma led the survey party across her fields for two miles to the site of the Rabbit Ears Campground, in the background. Some of her 1,000-head herd of cattle have caught the scent of the bales of hay in the back of her pickup and are closing in for a handout. Jere Krakow is at center, Leo Oliva at right.

A few yards to the right, the Canadian River enters a steep gorge. A hundred yards to the left, it flows over deep sand. Here, at the Rock Crossing of the Canadian, is the only place for a hundred miles where the Santa Fe wagons could cross. Leo Oliva is walking over the bed of solid rock toward the mesa on the east.

The right combination of clouds and shadows didn't materialize until thirty minutes after the camera was positioned. This is the famous Round Mound in New Mexico, known as Mount Clayton today.

There are three in Kansas, but there is only one Point of Rocks in New Mexico. It has strange fortifications in the upper reaches—spans of rock walls across the gorges. No one today knows their origin.

Sometimes, when the soil is sandy and porous, the ruts of the Santa Fe Trail start eroding. This is what the water did to a long stretch of the Santa Fe Trail near New Mexico's Point of Rocks.

The Sapello stage station, located on the bank of the Sapello (pronounced SAP-e-oh) Creek near Watrous, New Mexico, is original except for the porch. It has been occupied continuously since staging days.

When travelers along the Cimarron Cutoff could look ahead and see Wagon Mound on the horizon, they knew they were closing in on their goal, the city of Santa Fe.

The Watrous house and store at the junction of the Moro and Sapello streams is now the elegant headquarters of the Doolittle Ranch. The wing at left is the original structure; adobe additions enclose this courtyard.

The little community of Tiptonville grew up around the stage stop near Watrous. This is the old Tiptonville store, now in use as a farm outbuilding.

The town of San Miguel was established in the late eighteenth century, and its church, San Miguel del Vado, was built in 1805.

The church of San Jose del Vado stands in the center of a dusty, windswept plaza, in the decaying town of San Jose, New Mexico.

The Civil War Battle of Glorieta Pass centered on Pigeon's Ranch. This is the only building remaining from the ranch complex.

This ruin is all that is left of the old Pecos church, Nuestra Señora de Los Angeles de Porciúncula.

Dr. Marc Simmons, unchallenged as the nation's leading scholar of the Santa Fe Trail, stands among the earthen mounds of the remains of old Fort Marcy, overlooking Santa Fe. Simmons, seriously injured in an automobile accident in 1986, is winning a valiant fight to regain his health. He is the first president of the Santa Fe Trail Association.

Charles Bent, brother and partner of the builder of Bent's Old Fort, was killed during the Taos Uprising in 1847. He was still alive when an Indian wrapped a bowstring around his scalp and deftly popped it off. He is buried in the Santa Fe National Cemetery.

The Palace of the Governors dates back to Spanish colonial days and was easily the most important building in Santa Fe. Currently it houses the Museum of New Mexico.

The old Santa Fe Trail passed by the front door of the San Miguel Mission, two blocks from the Plaza in Santa Fe.

Kit Carson, the celebrated scout who left his imprint throughout the nineteenth century West, is buried in Taos.

There is a small cemetery in the churchyard at St. Francisco Asis, Taos, richly ornamented with religious icons. Behind the wall is an adobe squalor.

THE MOUNTAIN BRANCH

It is a six-mile drive from I-25 to old Fort Union, and all along the way are found the ruts of the Mountain Branch, the Cimarron Cutoff, or both.

Lucien Maxwell, who inherited the largest single piece of privately owned real estate in the United States, lived in the central portion of this residence in Rayado. The Maxwell Grant extended into the present states of New Mexico and Colorado.

The St. James Hotel is a classic case of being in the right place at the wrong time. An elegant hostelry, it was built in Cimarron, New Mexico, the booming town which grew up along the Mountain Branch of the Santa Fe Trail. But the year was 1880, one year after the railroad came over Raton Pass and ended the era of the Santa Fe Trail. Nevertheless, the hotel prospered for many years of the settlement era, then closed. It was carefully restored and reopened in 1975 by Ed and Pat Sitzberger, and is even more luxurious today than in its first period of life.

Mark Gardner tests the water at Willow Spring, now powered by an electric pump but still issuing the clear, cool water of trail days. It is in the backyard of a private home in Raton, New Mexico.

On the Canadian River, south of Raton Pass, there once stood a magnificent three-story adobe stage station known as Clifton House. This is all that is left today.

Those entering Raton Pass from the south can turn around and catch this breathtaking view of the valley of the Canadian River. The buildings of the city of Raton are in the foreground.

The Santa Fe Trail survey party was often the target of curious attention.

The Santa Fe Railroad erected this sign near the entrance to the tunnel which carries the railroad from Colorado to New Mexico.

Ruts of the Santa Fe Trail course along this row of trees in Raton Pass. In view to the northwest are the majestic Spanish Peaks.

The Raton Pass tunnel of the Atchison, Topeka and Santa Fe Railroad.

This adobe structure is all that is left of the buildings erected at the north entrance to Raton Pass by Richens Lacy (''Uncle Dick'') Wootton. This is now on the ranch of Don Berg.

This adobe barn at the Wootton Ranch was built in the first decade of the twentieth century by J. P. Morgan interests, when they owned the Raton Pass establishment.

The Baca House in Trinidad, Colorado, is a historic adobe structure owned and operated by the Colorado Historical Society.

Fisher's Peak originally was known to the traders as Raton Mountain. It towers majestically over Trinidad, Colorado.

Marion Russell was the author of *Land of Enchantment,* the story of her life as it revolved around the Santa Fe Trail. Soon after her husband's resignation from the U.S. Army, the Russells settled in the idyllic Stonewall area west of Trinidad. Here is that startling rock formation, the Stonewall.

As the Santa Fe Trail matured, a number of shortcuts developed. This old toll house is in New Mexico, south of Emery Gap, on the Military Road.

On the road to the picnic area of the John Martin Reservoir, south of Hasty, Colorado, is this curious rock formation atop a high stone hill. A Cheyenne brave named Red Shin incurred the enmity of his fellow Indians over a woman, was pursued, and mounted the platform atop the hill. From there he was able to defend himself successfully, and ever since it is been known as Red Shin's Standing Ground.

The swale of the Santa Fe Trail is broad and deep near the town of Hoehne, north of Trinidad, Colorado. Trouble is, it is filled with an awful assortment of junk.

Timpas Creek flows south of Bent's Old Fort, where it made a deep, narrow canyon with a rock floor. There was a hole in that floor filled with water, appropriately called Hole in the Rock, and a stage station by that name was built nearby. Then came the railroad which threw a dam across the canyon to trap water for their locomotives. The silt settled over the rock floor to a depth of six or more feet, and the Hole in the Rock now is lost forever.

The Iron Spring caused a stage station to be sited south of Bent's Old Fort. Now it is enclosed in concrete and keeps several stock tanks filled via underground piping.

William W. Bent, the St. Louis entrepreneur who founded Bent's Old Fort and became the West's leading Indian trader, is buried in the cemetery at Las Animas, Colorado.

There is no more dramatic structure on the plains today than the National Park Service's Bent's Old Fort, near Lamar, Colorado. This is how it looked on the dawn of May 16, 1988.

Kit Carson became deathly ill on a stage trip from the railhead at Cheyenne to his home in Taos, and left the vehicle at Boggsville. He was carried to the surgeon's quarters at the new Fort Lyon, Colorado, and died here. The building is now the Kit Carson Chapel; only the stone walls are original.

A fur press is the focus in the courtyard of Bent's Old Fort. This is a shining example of the way the National Park Service can restore a historical structure with authentic detail.

Boggsville is now a two-building town, south of Las Animas, Colorado. John Wesley Prowers built one of the two remaining adobe houses; this one was the home of Thomas O. Boggs. The structures now are owned by the Bent County Historical Society, which needs financial assistance to help pay for stabilization and restoration.

William Bent burned his old fort and built a new one, still on the Arkansas but far to the east. The site is just north of the ghost town of Prowers. All that remains today is this array of foundation stones.

The survey party inspects the site of Old Fort Lyon with the aid of a historical plat provided by Paul Bentrup. From left: Jere Krakow, Bentrup, Leo Oliva, John Paige, Don Hill of Fort Union, and Tom Betz of the Lamar *Daily News*.

Paul Bentrup, right, a dogged researcher from Deerfield, Kansas, shows Jere Krakow the ruts on the Foulks Ranch near Garden City, Kansas.

The bridge over the Arkansas River at Las Animas proved an ideal vantage point for studying the shallow, braided stream.

Other Western Books Marketed by The Patrice Press

Following the Santa Fe Trail, Marc Simmons, Ph.D. 214 pages. Paper, $12.95

Images of the Santa Fe Trail, Gregory M. Franzwa. 114 photographs. Cloth, $24.95, ISBN: 0-935284-60-5. Paper, $19.95, ISBN: 0-935284-61-3.

Impressions of The Santa Fe Trail: A Contemporary Diary, Gregory M. Franzwa. 200 pages. Cloth, $14.95, ISBN: 0-935284-62-1. Paper, $9.95, ISBN: 0-935284-63-X.

Land of Enchantment; Memoirs of Marian Russell along the Santa Fe Trail, ed. by Garnet M. Brayer. 163 pages. Paper, $12.95

The Santa Fe Trail; The National Park Service 1963 Historic Sites Survey, William E. Brown. 221 pages. Cloth, $17.95, ISBN: 0-935284-64-8.

Exploring the American West, 1803-1879, William Goetzmann. 128 pages. Paper, $7.95

Indian, Soldier, and Settler, Robert M. Utley. 84 pages. Paper, $7.95

Kansas in Maps, Robert W. Baughman. 104 pages. Cloth, $14.95

The Beginning of the West, Louise Barry. 1296 pages. Cloth, $14.75

The Latter-day Saints' Emigrants' Guide, Wm. Clayton; Stanley B. Kimball, Ph.D., ed. 107 pages. Paper, $19.95, ISBN: 0-935284-27-3.

The Overland Migrations, David Lavender. 111 pages. Paper, $7.95

Emigrant Trails West, Helfrich/Hunt. 211 pages. Paper, $19.95

Fort Laramie, David Lavender. 159 pages. Paper, $8.95

Fort Vancouver, David Lavender. 143 pages. Paper, $8.95

Forty-niners, Archer Butler Hulbert. 340 pages. Paper, $14.95

Ghost Trails to California, Tom Hunt. 288 pages, 8½″ x 11″. Cloth, $34.95; paper, $22.95

Historic Sites Along the Oregon Trail, Aubrey L. Haines. 439 pages. Cloth, $24.95, ISBN: 0-935284-50-8. Paper, $12.95, ISBN: 0-935284-51-6.

Historic Sites and Markers Along the Mormon and Other Great Western Trails, Stanley B. Kimball. 320 pages. Cloth, $37.95; paper, $15.95.

Maps of the Oregon Trail, Gregory M. Franzwa. 292 pages. Cloth, $24.95, ISBN: 0-935284-30-3. Paper, $14.95, ISBN: 0-935284-32-X. Looseleaf, $27.95, ISBN: 0-935284-31-1.

Oregon Trail map 16″X 24″ $2.95

Overland to California with the Pioneer Line; The Gold Rush Diary of Bernard K. Reid, ed. by Mary McDougall Gordon. 246 pages. Paper, $14.95

Platte River Road Narratives, Merrill J. Mattes. 672 pages, 8½″ x 11″. Cloth, $95

Pump on the Prairie, Musetta Gilman. 223 pages. Paper, $12.95

Scotts Bluff, Merrill J. Mattes. 64 pages. Paper, $2.45

The Great Platte River Road, Merrill J. Mattes. 583 pages. Cloth, $36.95; paper, $16.95

The Oregon Trail Revisited, Gregory M. Franzwa. 419 pages. Cloth, $14.95, ISBN: 0-935284-57-5. Paper, $7.95, ISBN: 0-935284-58-3.

The Wake of the Prairie Schooner, Irene D. Paden. 514 pages. Cloth, $24.95, ISBN: 0-935284-40-0. Paper, $12.95, ISBN: 0-935284-38-9.

Trail of the First Wagons Over the Sierra Nevada, Charles K. Graydon. 81 pages. Paper, $12.95, ISBN: 0-935284-47-8

To the Land of Gold and Wickedness: The 1848-59 Diary of Lorena Hays, Jeanne Watson, ed. 496 pages. Cloth, $27.95, ISBN: 0-935284-53-2.

Whitman Mission, Erwin N. Thompson. 92 pages. Paper, $4.45

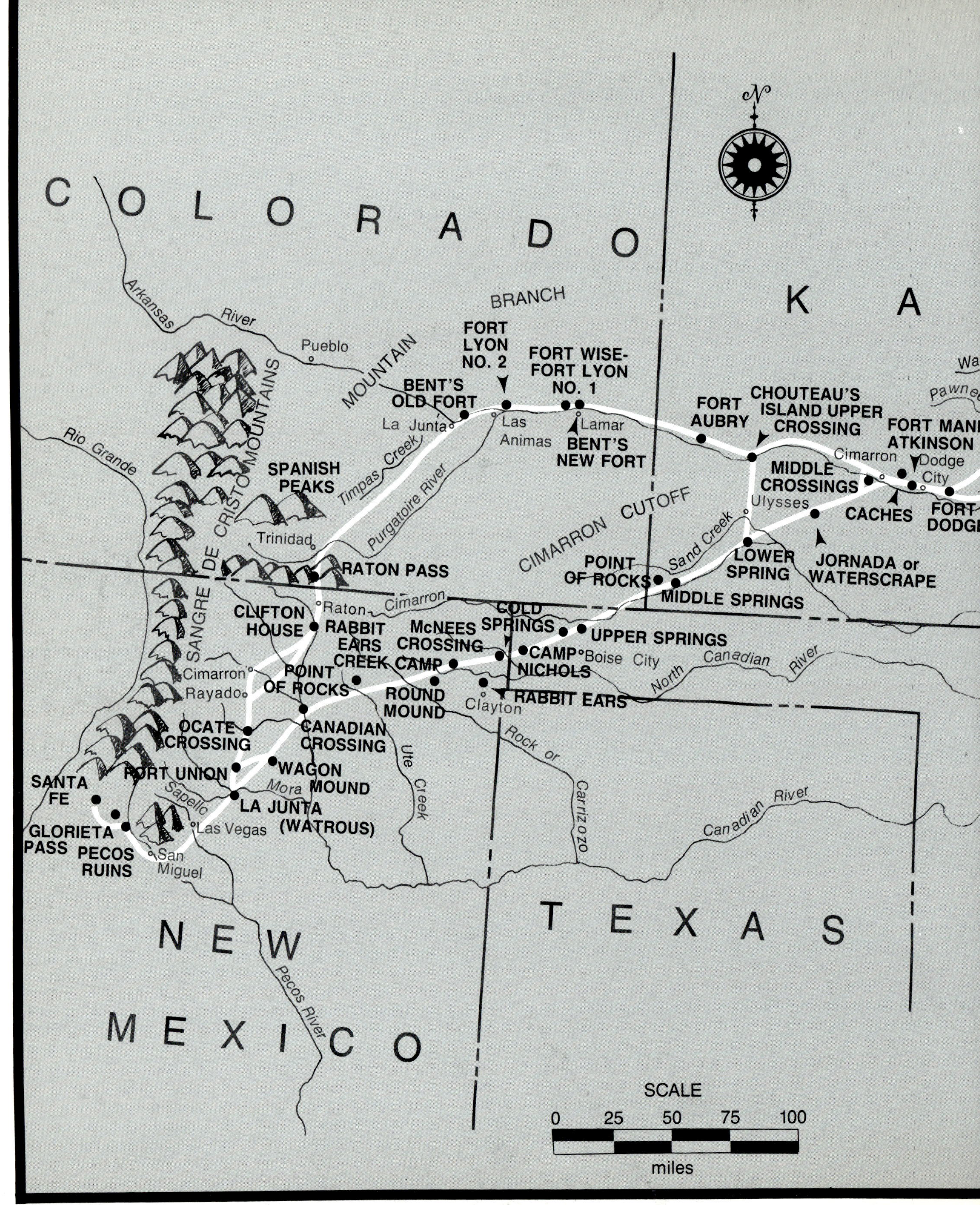

COLORADO
KA
TEXAS
NEW MEXICO
MOUNTAIN BRANCH
CIMARRON CUTOFF
Arkansas River
Pueblo
SANGRE DE CRISTO MOUNTAINS
BENT'S OLD FORT
FORT LYON NO. 2
FORT WISE-FORT LYON NO. 1
La Junta
Las Animas
Lamar
BENT'S NEW FORT
FORT AUBRY
CHOUTEAU'S ISLAND UPPER CROSSING
FORT MANN
ATKINSON
Dodge City
Cimarron
MIDDLE CROSSINGS
CACHES
FORT DODGE
Ulysses
JORNADA or WATERSCRAPE
Pawnee
Rio Grande
SPANISH PEAKS
Timpas Creek
Purgatoire River
Trinidad
RATON PASS
POINT OF ROCKS
Sand Creek
LOWER SPRING
MIDDLE SPRINGS
Raton
Cimarron
CLIFTON HOUSE
RABBIT EARS CREEK CAMP
McNEES CROSSING
COLD SPRINGS
UPPER SPRINGS
CAMP NICHOLS
Boise City
North Canadian River
Cimarron
Rayado
POINT OF ROCKS
ROUND MOUND
Clayton
RABBIT EARS
OCATE CROSSING
CANADIAN CROSSING
Ute Creek
Rock or Carrizozo
FORT UNION
WAGON MOUND
Mora
Sapello
LA JUNTA (WATROUS)
SANTA FE
GLORIETA PASS
PECOS RUINS
Las Vegas
San Miguel
Canadian River
Pecos River
SCALE
0 25 50 75 100
miles